# Ramadan

## Festivals Around the World

Words in **bold** can be found
in the glossary on page 24.

©2016
Book Life
King's Lynn
Norfolk PE30 4LS

ISBN: 978-1-910512-97-5

All rights reserved. Printed in Spain

**Written by:**
Grace Jones

**Designed by:**
Matt Rumbelow

A catalogue record for this book
is available from the British Library.

# Ramadan

**Festivals Around the World**

Hello, my name is Noor.

When you see Noor, she will tell you how to say a word.

# What is a Festival?

A festival takes place when people come together to celebrate a special event or time of the year. Some festivals last for only one day and others

Some people celebrate festivals by having a party with their family and friends. Others celebrate by holding special events, performing dances or playing music.

# What is Islam?

Islam is a **religion** that began over one thousand years ago in the Middle East. **Muslims** believe in one God, called Allah, who they pray to in a mosque or Muslim place of **worship**.

A MOSQUE IN ISTANBUL.

Muslims read a holy book called the **Qur'an**. The Qur'an is Allah's word and instructs people on how to practice their **faith**. An **imam** teaches people about Allah's word and leads prayers in the mosque.

Noor says:
MOSK (Mosque)
KUR-AN (Qur'an)

# What is Ramadan?

Ramadan is a festival celebrated by Muslims for one month of every year. Ramadan is a time when Muslims **fast** for one month during the daylight hours.

Noor says:
RAM-A-DAN (Ramadan)

During fasting hours, Muslims do not eat or drink, but at night time they are allowed to. At Ramadan, Muslims celebrate their faith in Allah through prayer and worship.

Ramadan is celebrated in the ninth month of the Islamic calendar.

# The Story of Ramadan

A long, long time ago, there once was a man called Muhammad. He walked the desert day and night thinking about his faith in Allah (God). One night, a voice called to Muhammad from the sky. It said "You have been chosen to hear Allah's words".

Allah spoke to Muhammad and told him how to practice his faith and lead a good life. Muhammad spread Allah's word to other people. They were written down in a holy book so all Muslims could follow them. This book was called the Qur'an.

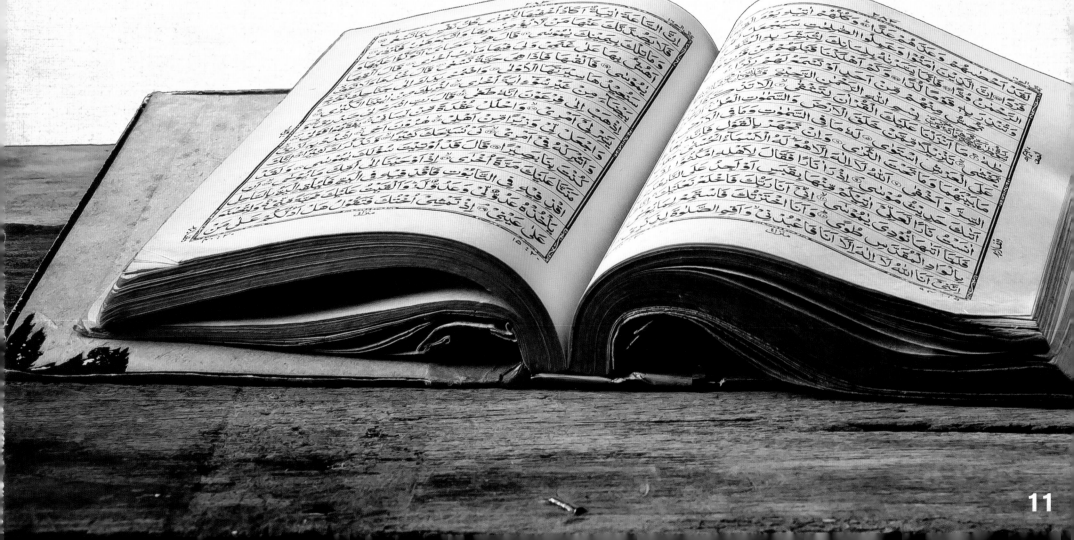

# Festival of Fasting

Muslims fast during the month of Ramadan because it was in this month that Allah passed on his word to Muhammad. At nightime, Muslims can eat and drink as much as they like. There are many markets and food stalls open until late into the night.

Fasting is called 'Sawm' in Arabic.

Before the sun rises, Muslims have a breakfast meal called **Suhoor** and when the sun sets, they have an evening meal called the **Iftar**.

People wish each other "Ramadan Mubarak" which means "have a blessed Ramadan".

Noor says:
SUH-OAR **(Suhoor)**
IF-TA **(Iftar)**

A traditional Suhoor meal.

# Why do Muslims
# Fast during Ramadan?

Ramadan is a time for people to celebrate and remember their faith in Allah. When fasting ends for the day, Muslims often go to their friends and families houses to pray together.

The festival is also a time to remember others who may be hungry and less fortunate than themselves. By fasting for one month, Muslims feel what it is like to be hungry and poor like many other people in the world.

# Prayer and Worship

In the evenings, Muslims attend special nightime prayers, called **Tarawih** prayers at their local mosque. Tarawih prayers only take place during Ramadan.

Noor says:
TAR-AH-WEAR (Tarawih)

Each night during Ramadan, a part of the Qur'an is read aloud. By the end of the month, the whole of the holy book has been read aloud.

# Eid ul-Fitr

At the end of the month of Ramadan, another festival, called **Eid ul-Fitr** takes place. It is a time when fasting stops and people are allowed to eat in the daytime.

**Noor says:**
EEDUL-FIR-TRA (Eid ul-Fitr)

Families and friends come together to eat a special meal, exchange gifts and dress in their best clothes.

Eid ul-Fitr lasts for only one day.

# Family and Friends

Ramadan and Eid ul-Fitr are both festivals that celebrate sharing and forgiveness. People give money to others that don't have enough so they can celebrate these special festivals too. This is called Zakat ul-Fitr.

Although Muslim's celebrate their faith in Allah during the festival, Ramadan is also about spending time with family, friends and loved ones.

Noor says:
ZA-KAT UL-FIR-TRA (Zakat ul-Fitr)

# or Says...

**Eid ul-Fitr**

**EED UL-FIR-TRA**

Another festival celebrated by Muslims
that takes place at the end of Ramadan.

**Iftar**

**IF-TA**

An evening meal eaten during Ramadan.

**Mosque**

**MOSK**

A mosque is a Muslim place of worship.

**Qur'an**

**KUR-AN**

The Qur'an is the writing of Allah's word in a holy book.